MY GRANDPA'S FULL NAME: _____

DATE OF BIRTH: _____

PLACE OF BIRTH: _____

MY GRANDPA'S MOTHER'S FULL NAME: _____

DATE OF BIRTH: _____

PLACE OF BIRTH: _____

MY GRANDPA'S FATHER'S FULL NAME: _____

DATE OF BIRTH: _____

PLACE OF BIRTH: _____

GRANDPA, YOUR LIFE IS A GIFT.

YOU HOLD WITHIN YOU A STORY THAT ONLY YOU CAN SHARE. USE THESE PAGES TO FILL WITH YOUR ONE-OF-A-KIND MEMORIES—WHETHER IT'S A SPECIAL MOMENT FROM YOUR CHILDHOOD, INFORMATION ABOUT YOUR HERITAGE, AN UNFORGETTABLE ADVENTURE, OR A PIECE OF ADVICE TO PASS ON.

SPEAK FROM THE HEART, IN YOUR OWN WORDS—IT DOESN'T NEED TO BE FORMAL OR COMPLEX. BECAUSE WHEN YOU ARE FINISHED, YOU WILL CREATE A GIFT THAT WILL BE LOVED FOR GENERATIONS.

PAST GENERATIONS

WHAT ARE SOME STORIES ABOUT YOUR OWN GRANDPARENTS?
WHERE WERE THEY BORN? DO YOU REMEMBER WHAT THEY
LOOKED LIKE? WHAT WERE THEIR PERSONALITIES LIKE?

FAMILY FACES ARE MAGIC MIRRORS. LOOKING AT PEOPLE WHO BELONG TO US, WE SEE THE PAST, PRESENT, AND FUTURE.

GAIL LUMET BUCKLEY

SENTIMENTAL KEEPSAKES

WHAT ARE SOME FAMILY HEIRLOOMS OR MEMENTOS YOU'VE
KEPT? WHY ARE THEY SPECIAL TO YOU?

_____

_____

_____

_____

_____

_____

_____

FAMILY RELATIONSHIPS

WHAT WAS YOUR RELATIONSHIP WITH YOUR PARENTS LIKE?
DID YOU HAVE SPECIAL RELATIONSHIPS WITH ANY OTHER
FAMILY MEMBERS?

JOYS OF CHILDHOOD

PLACES YOU LIKED TO PLAY GROWING UP:

FAVORITE FAMILY MEALS OR RECIPES:

SCHOOL SUBJECTS THAT YOU LOVED:

BEING A KID

WHAT DO YOU MISS MOST ABOUT BEING A KID? IT COULD BE A SPECIFIC ACTIVITY OR PERHAPS A FEELING YOU MISS.

_____

_____

_____

_____

_____

_____

_____

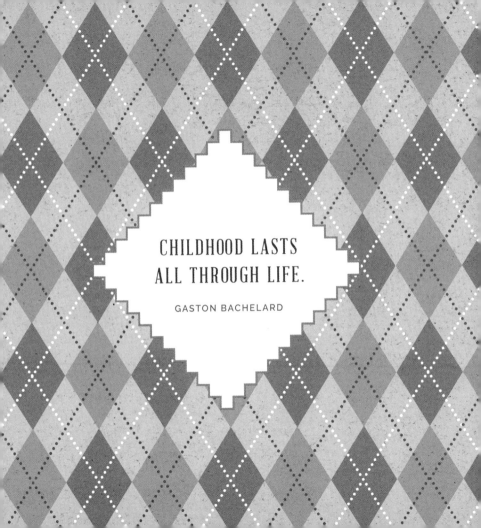

CHILDHOOD LASTS
ALL THROUGH LIFE.

GASTON BACHELARD

FIRST MEMORIES

MY EARLIEST MEMORY IS:

WHEN I WAS LITTLE, I WOULD GET TO SCHOOL BY:

AS A CHILD, I WAS AFRAID OF:

MY FAVORITE TOYS WERE:

I'VE ALWAYS HAD A NATURAL TALENT FOR:

SOME OF THE CHORES I HAD GROWING UP WERE:

GENE PERRET

CHILDHOOD HOME

WHAT WAS YOUR HOME LIKE GROWING UP? INCLUDE DETAILS ABOUT
THE NEIGHBORHOOD, WHO LIVED WITH YOU, WHAT YOUR ROOM WAS
LIKE, AND HOW AND WHERE YOUR FAMILY SPENT TIME TOGETHER.

MUSIC, MOVIES, BOOKS

FAVORITE CHILDHOOD BOOKS:

FAVORITE CHILDHOOD MOVIES:

FAVORITE CHILDHOOD MUSIC:

FAVORITE CHILDHOOD GAMES OR SPORTS:

FAVORITE CHILDHOOD HOBBIES, INTERESTS,
OR COLLECTIONS:

SIBLINGS & FRIENDSHIPS

WHAT WAS YOUR RELATIONSHIP WITH YOUR SIBLINGS LIKE, AND WHAT STORIES DO YOU REMEMBER ABOUT THEM? YOU CAN ALSO DESCRIBE CHILDHOOD FRIENDS AND THE ADVENTURES YOU HAD TOGETHER.

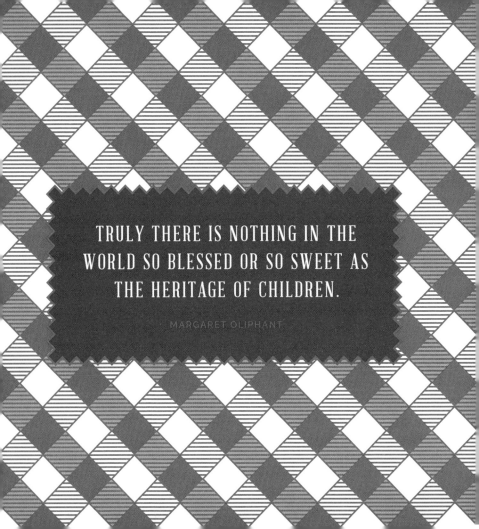

TRULY THERE IS NOTHING IN THE WORLD SO BLESSED OR SO SWEET AS THE HERITAGE OF CHILDREN.

MARGARET OLIPHANT

COST OF LIVING

HOW MUCH DID THESE COST WHEN YOU WERE GROWING UP?

A GALLON OF MILK _____

A MOVIE TICKET _____

A NEW CAR _____

YOUR FIRST PAYING JOB WAS:

HOW OLD YOU WERE WHEN YOU STARTED:

HOW MUCH YOU WERE PAID:

TIME TRAVEL

IF YOU COULD GO BACK IN TIME TO RELIVE ANY MOMENT IN
YOUR LIFE, WHAT WOULD IT BE AND WHY?

_____

_____

_____

_____

_____

_____

_____

...HISTORY ISN'T JUST
THE PAST. IT'S ALIVE IN US.

NATALIE PORTMAN

DEFINING SUCCESS

WHAT DOES SUCCESS MEAN TO YOU?

WHO ARE SOME PEOPLE YOU BELIEVE ARE SUCCESSFUL?

HOW HAVE YOU BEEN SUCCESSFUL?

ONE OF THE MOST POWERFUL HANDCLASPS IS THAT
OF A NEW GRANDBABY AROUND THE FINGER OF A
GRANDFATHER.

JOY HARGROVE

BEING A FATHER

WHAT WAS IT LIKE TO BECOME A FATHER? WHAT ARE
SOME OF YOUR VERY FIRST MEMORIES OF YOUR CHILDREN?

_____

_____

_____

_____

_____

_____

_____

CLEVER INVENTIONS

THINGS THAT HAVE BEEN CREATED AFTER YOU
HAD CHILDREN THAT YOU WISH YOU HAD:

HOLIDAY TRADITIONS

WHAT WAS YOUR FAVORITE HOLIDAY TO CELEBRATE WHEN
YOUR CHILDREN WERE GROWING UP? WHAT WERE SOME
HOLIDAY TRADITIONS THAT YOU HAD?

_____

_____

_____

_____

_____

_____

_____

GRANDPARENTS ARE A FAMILY'S
GREATEST TREASURE, THE FOUNDERS OF
A LOVING LEGACY...

UNKNOWN

LITTLE RASCALS

LIST TIMES WHEN YOUR OWN CHILDREN DID SOMETHING
THAT DROVE YOU CRAZY OR TESTED FAMILY RULES:

_____

_____

_____

_____

_____

_____

_____

SIGNS OF AFFECTION

HOW DO YOU SHOW YOUR LOVE TO YOUR CHILDREN OR GRANDCHILDREN?
DO YOU SHOWER THEM WITH GIFTS? PRAISE THEIR SUCCESSES? MAYBE
YOU GENTLY ENCOURAGE THEM TO DO THEIR BEST OR HAVE A SPECIAL
TRADITION JUST BETWEEN YOU. SHARE YOUR THOUGHTS HERE:

_____

_____

_____

_____

_____

_____

_____

BY GIVING CHILDREN LOTS
OF AFFECTION, YOU CAN HELP FILL
THEM WITH LOVE AND
ACCEPTANCE OF THEMSELVES.

WAYNE DYER

WORDS TO REMEMBER

THINGS YOU'VE OFTEN SAID TO YOUR
CHILDREN OR GRANDCHILDREN:

THINGS YOUR CHILDREN OR GRANDCHILDREN
HAVE SAID THAT YOU'LL NEVER FORGET:

_____

_____

_____

_____

_____

_____

_____

...WHEN I EMBRACE MY

GRANDFATHER

I EXPERIENCE A SENSE OF RICHNESS AS THOUGH I AM
A NOTE IN THE HEARTBEATS OF THE VERY UNIVERSE.

TAYEB SALIH

IMPRESSIVE CHILDREN

IN WHAT WAYS DO YOUR CHILDREN OR GRANDCHILDREN
MAKE YOU PROUD?

FAVORITES

ONE OF YOUR FAVORITE COLORS IS:

MOST DAYS, YOU'RE WEARING:

YOUR FAVORITE DESSERT IS:

A SMELL THAT MAKES YOU STOP EVERY TIME IS:

YOU LOVE PLAYING THIS GAME:

A BOOK THAT HAS STUCK WITH YOU IS:

MUSIC YOU LOVE TO LISTEN TO IS:

YOUR FAVORITE MOVIE OF ALL TIME IS:

YOU'RE HAPPIEST WHEN YOU ARE:

WORDS YOU TRY TO LIVE BY ARE:

BEING A GRANDFATHER

WHAT WAS IT LIKE TO BECOME A GRANDFATHER? HOW HAS IT AFFECTED YOUR RELATIONSHIP WITH YOUR OWN CHILDREN?

_____

_____

_____

_____

_____

_____

_____

FORTUNATE ARE
THE PEOPLE WHOSE
ROOTS ARE DEEP.

AGNES MEYER

YOUR BEST QUALITIES

WHAT ARE SOME THINGS PEOPLE OFTEN
COMPLIMENT YOU ON?

_____

_____

_____

_____

_____

_____

_____

WHICH ONE MEANS THE MOST TO YOU AND WHY?

PERSONALITY TRAITS

WHAT ABOUT YOU HAS STAYED THE SAME THROUGHOUT
YOUR LIFE? WHAT'S CHANGED?

_____

_____

_____

_____

_____

_____

_____

[KIDS] DON'T REMEMBER WHAT YOU TRY TO TEACH THEM. THEY REMEMBER WHAT YOU ARE.

JIM HENSON

LIFE MOTTO

WHAT IS YOUR FAVORITE QUOTE OR SAYING? OR MAYBE
YOU HAVE SEVERAL? SHARE THEM HERE AND DESCRIBE
WHAT THEY MEAN TO YOU.

_____

_____

_____

_____

_____

_____

NOBODY CAN DO FOR
LITTLE CHILDREN WHAT
GRANDPARENTS DO.

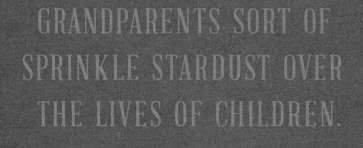

GRANDPARENTS SORT OF
SPRINKLE STARDUST OVER
THE LIVES OF CHILDREN.

ALEX HALEY

WORLD EVENTS

WHAT MAJOR EVENTS HAVE YOU WITNESSED IN YOUR LIFE?
WHERE WERE YOU AND HOW DID THEY AFFECT YOU?

GOING PLACES

LIST PLACES YOU'VE TRAVELED TO SO FAR:

_____

_____

_____

_____

_____

_____

_____

LIST PLACES YOU'D LIKE TO TRAVEL TO:

LIFE LESSONS

WHAT HAVE BEEN SOME OF THE HARDEST CHALLENGES
FOR YOU IN LIFE? HOW HAVE THEY AFFECTED YOU?
WHAT DID YOU LEARN OR GAIN FROM THEM?

_____

_____

_____

_____

_____

_____

_____

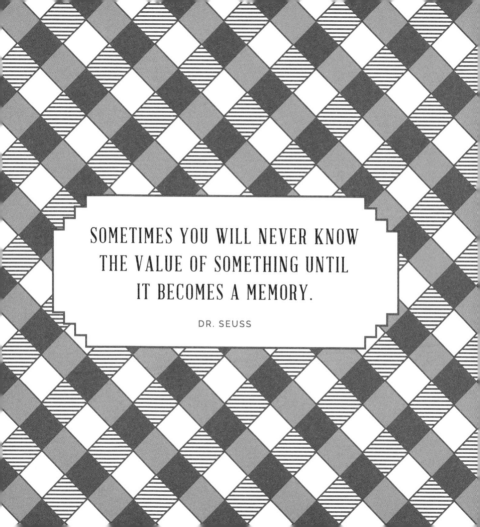

SOMETIMES YOU WILL NEVER KNOW
THE VALUE OF SOMETHING UNTIL
IT BECOMES A MEMORY.

DR. SEUSS

THREE THINGS

3 THINGS YOU'RE PROUD OF:

_____

_____

_____

3 THINGS YOU'RE PASSIONATE ABOUT:

_____

_____

_____

3 THINGS YOU'VE LOST:

_____

_____

_____

3 THINGS YOU LOOK FORWARD TO:

_____

_____

_____

LIFE BRINGS SIMPLE PLEASURES TO US
EVERY DAY. IT IS UP TO US TO MAKE THEM

WONDERFUL
MEMORIES.

CATHY ALLEN

FUTURE DREAMS

WHAT ARE SOME THINGS YOU HAVE YET TO DO AND
WOULD LIKE TO ACCOMPLISH IN YOUR LIFETIME?

_____

_____

_____

_____

_____

_____

_____

ROLE MODELS

WHO DID YOU LOOK UP TO AS A CHILD AND WHY?

_____

_____

_____

_____

_____

_____

_____

WHO DO YOU LOOK UP TO NOW AND WHY?

_____

_____

_____

_____

_____

_____

_____

SOUND ADVICE

IF YOU COULD PASS ALONG ONE PIECE OF ADVICE,
WHAT WOULD IT BE?

A LOVING HEART IS
THE TRUEST WISDOM.

CHARLES DICKENS

GIVING THANKS

LIST 10 THINGS YOU'RE GRATEFUL FOR IN YOUR LIFE:

GRANDFATHER JOYS

WHAT'S THE BEST (OR MOST FUN) THING ABOUT BEING
A GRANDFATHER? WHAT ARE SOME THINGS YOU LOVE ABOUT
YOUR GRANDCHILDREN?

A LASTING WISH

WHAT WISHES DO YOU HAVE FOR YOUR CHILDREN
AND GRANDCHILDREN?

WHEN YOU LOOK AT YOUR LIFE,
THE GREATEST HAPPINESSES
ARE FAMILY HAPPINESSES.

JOYCE BROTHERS

COMPENDIUM®
Live inspired

WITH SPECIAL THANKS TO THE ENTIRE COMPENDIUM FAMILY.

CREDITS:
WRITTEN BY: MIRIAM HATHAWAY
DESIGNED BY: JESSICA PHOENIX
EDITED BY: AMELIA RIEDLER

ISBN: 978-1-943200-45-0

4TH PRINTING. PRINTED IN CHINA WITH SOY AND METALLIC INKS ON FSC®-CERTIFIED PAPER.